"Taking a refreshing approach to life coaching, Mike 'Ambassador' Bruny's 'Move the Crowd' offers 30 days of powerful anecdotes taken from the lyrics of notable MCs to Challenge readers to move towards positive self-motivation." **~The Source Magazine: The Bible of Hip-Hop Music, Culture & Politics**

"Ambassador Bruny you're the man for this one, your book, 'Move the Crowd,' is very inspirational and keeps me on point. I finished reading it a while ago but still crack it open daily. The question of the day is another element of the book that I love. Keep up the great work and I look forward to your next release." **~ DJ Whutevva; Power105.1 FM, NYC**

"With 'Move the Crowd,' expert life coach and motivational speaker, Mike Bruny offers practical steps to finding to finding the motivation to accomplish desires, goals and dreams. This 30 day journey is full of wisdom and inspiration."
~Emmett G. Price III Ph.D; Chair, Department of African-American Studies, Northeastern University

"'Move the Crowd' is an excellent addition to the vast amount of writing on hip-hop. This goes one step further and uses the lyrics of artists to help us (hip-hop lovers) focus our minds and dig deep to bring about positive changes in our lives. If you are looking for a change and you love hip-hop, pick up this book and Move the Crowds within your life."
~Don C. Sawyer, III; Syracuse University

"I loved how classic hip hop artist lyric's were tied in on issues that happen daily."
~Sonia T.; University of Massachusetts, Amherst

"I am big into hip hop, so I have to admit that it was nice reading something positive about hip hop and how it can actually help its listeners as well as attract new ones." **~Najee S. (Stony Brook U.)**

"I thought the 'Move the Crowd' was great. I thought it was a great tribute to hip hop and all its positivity." **~Louis D.; University of South Carolina**

"When most people think of rap, they immediately think negatively. After reading, 'Move the Crowd,' I thought how positive these lyrics really are."
~Yolanda Wyns, Recording Artist, Vocal Coach; YWYNS ENTERTAINMENT

Move the Crowd

30 Days of Hip Hop Affirmations to Change Your Life

Mike Bruny

authorHOUSE®

AuthorHouse™
1663 Liberty Drive
Bloomington, IN 47403
www.authorhouse.com
Phone: 1-800-839-8640

First published by AuthorHouse 3/26/2010

ISBN: 978-1-4389-3965-0 (sc)

Printed in the United States of America
Bloomington, Indiana

This book is printed on acid-free paper.

Dedication

To my wife, Ji-eun:

You inspire me to think big and live even bigger.

Without you this book would have become a fleeting thought in the basement of my mind.

Love You.

"I'm a movement by myself, but I'm a force when we're together, mommy I'm good all by myself, but baby you, you make me better."

~Fabolous featuring Neyo [Song: Make me Better]

And

To my nephew Jonathan aka Little Johnny:

You are the original author of the family and I look forward to all the great books that you will create for the world.   Thanks for the inspiration and your imagination.

The present is yours!

"So listen, be strong, scream 'whoopee-doo,' go for yours, 'cause dreams come true."

~Slick Rick [Song: Hey Young World]

v

Supporters
(Good looking out)

Thank you:

GOD for life, the idea for this book and for providing the necessary people to help bring it to life.

Those who previewed and provided feedback during the early stages; Dr. Emmett Price, Reverend Benjamin Abrahams, Joel Louis, Hans Momplaisir, Adrian Ford, Wayne Willis, Don Sawyer, Doshea Gordon, Luis Inoa, Garfield Drummond, Omar Mckenzie, Nyota Wright, Colleen Plummer, DJ Rey Garcia, Amira

To a few folks who believed in me before I believed in myself: Leo Smith, Andre Taylor, Jieun Yoo, Rev. Benjamin Abrahams, Mom & Dad.

A special thank you to Dr. Emmett Price who served as my editor, guide and fan.

Forward

In life there are three crowds of people: leaders, followers and spectators. Which crowd are you in?

Move the Crowd is an exceptional gift to the world. In it expert life coach and motivational trainer, Mike Bruny, offers more than daily affirmations to inspire and motivate positive outcomes; Mike offers a roadmap to life-changing transformation. Using lyrics from some of the most noted and popular Hip Hop MCs, Mike takes the reader on a journey of self-reflection and self-inquiry. A journey that challenges the crowd to Move!

In a world filled with negativity, chaos and stress, it is often difficult to find the motivation to think positive. The half-full glass consistently looks half-empty. **Move the Crowd** challenges the reader to STOP, ASSESS and MOVE in the desired direction. **Move the Crowd** is a powerful, potent, inspirational source of encouragement, motivation and affirmation. This pocket-sized, portable life manual is full of priceless nuggets of wisdom taken from Mike's own intimate experiences and shared with the fullest integrity, dignity and passion. **Move the Crowd** is a timely necessity!

Mike Bruny is prepared to aid you in reaching your maximum potential. Let him affirm the value of your dreams and visions. Let him help you to find joy, happiness, security, sanity and peace in life. Let him help you reach your goals, accomplish your feats and reach new heights in life. With Move the Crowd, Coach Mike blows the whistle...

... are you ready to move?

Emmett G. Price III, Ph.D.
Chair, Department of African-
American Studies
Northeastern University

Contents

Playlist		xiv
Preface		xvi
The Flow		xviii
Day 1	Winning	1
Day 2	Your Music	3
Day 3	My Gift to the World	5
Day 4	Vision	7
Day 5	Faith	9
Day 6	Support	11
Day 7	Tribulation	13
Day 8	Listening	15
Day 9	My Direction	18
Day 10	Opportunity	20
Day 11	Progress	22
Day 12	Love	24
Day 13	Preconceived Notion	27
Day 14	Your Mindset	29
Day 15	Your True Self	31
Day 16	Stress	34
Day 17	Attitude	36
Day 18	Being Worthy	38
Day 19	Make the Change	42
Day 20	Rejection	45

Day 21	Worry	47
Day 22	Passion	50
Day 23	Time Management	53
Day 24	Change	56
Day 25	Personal Expression	59
Day 26	Decision Making	61
Day 27	Focus	64
Day 28	A Fulfilling Life	66
Day 29	Staying Positive	70
Day 30	Transferable Skills	73

The Play List

Location	Song	Artist	Album
Cover	Move the Crowd	Rakim	The 18th Letter/The Book Of Life
Day 1	Change the Game	jay-Z,feat. Beanie Sigel & Memphis Bleek	The Dynasty: Roc La Familia
Day 2	The People	Common	Finding Forever
Day 3	Umi Says	Mos Def	Black on Both Sides
Day 4	Heart of the City(Ain't no love)	Jay-Z	The Blueprint
Day 5	In Due Time	OutKast Ft. Cee-Lo	Soul Food Sound Track
Day 6	Jesus Walks	Kanye West	The College Dropout
Day 7	I Try	Talib Kwali	Beautiful Struggle
Day 8	You Don't Know	Jay-Z	The Blueprint
Day 9	I Just Wanna Love U	Jay-z	The Dynasty: Roc La Familia
Day 10	Lose Yourself	Eminem	8 Mile Soundtrack
Day 11	Umi Says	Mos Def	Black on Both Sides
Day 12	21 Questions	50 Cent	Get Rich or Die Tryin'
Day 13	What More Can I Say	Jay-Z	The Black Album
Day 14	Diamonds from Sierra Leone (Remix)	Kanye West feat. Jay-Z	Late Registration

Day	Song	Artist	Album
Day 15	Lucky Me	Jay-Z	In my Lifetime, Vol.1
Day 16	Stressed Out	Tribe called Quest Ft. Faith Evans	Beats, Rhymes and Life
Day 17	If I Can't	50 Cent	Get Rich or Die Tryin'
Day 18	The World is Yours	Nas	Illmatic
Day 19	Hey Young World	Slick Rick	The Great Adventures of Slick Rick
Day 20	I Got a Man	Positive K	The Skills that Pay the Bills
Day 21	Did You Ever Think	R.Kelly	R.
Day 22	My First Song	Jay-Z	The Black Album
Day 23	Ghetto Prisoners	Nas	I am
Day 24	Free Style on hot 97	Jay-Z	http://www.defsounds.com/singles/Jay_z_hot_97_funkmaster_flex_freestyle
Day 25	Doo Wop (That Thing)	Lauryn Hill	The miseducation of lauryn hill
Day 26	Renegade	Jay-Z feat. Eminem	The Blueprint
Day 27	Best of Me (part two)	Mya ft. Jay-Z	Backstage: A Hard Knock Life Soundtrack
Day 28	The whole world looking at me	Busta Rhymes	When Disaster Strikes
Day 29	Doo Wop (That Thing)	Lauryn Hill	The miseducation of lauryn hill
Day 30	Everything I am	Kanye West	Graduation

Preface

It has been quite a journey to make "Move the Crowd: 30 Days of Hip Hop Affirmations to Change Your Life" transform from a concept in my mind to the words that are in this book. In line with my thought, "The sun is always shining behind the clouds," I've always been able to pull something positive out of what has been generalized as negative.

The duality of human beings is evident in this book. My goal is not to interpret what the artist meant, but to express how I interpreted and use it in a positive way.

Being born and raised in Brooklyn, NY, I take a certain level of pride in the words, "hip hop" and "rap." Just say, "where's Brooklyn at?" and my demeanor changes as I respond, "RIGHT HERE!"

The goal of "Move the Crowd" is to provide my readers with portable affirmations based on hip hop lyrics that have literally moved the writer.

My audience is those who find themselves covering their mouth with one of their hands, going, "Yo, you heard that" and quickly rewinding their tape deck (now shuffling ipods or mp3 players). I grew up with hip hop and I believe it grew up with me. Hip hop has gone from break dancing to beat boxing to corporate sponsorship and licensing. Hip hop's transitions have followed me from the Flatbush section of Brooklyn to a life coach and principal of Run the Point Enterprises to my first book.

May this book remind you how great you are and how great you can be. "Don't die with your music still inside you." ~Dr. Wayne Dyer

The Flow

"The Flow," includes suggestions on how to use this book. You could read through the book in one sitting if you really wanted to or use it as a daily guide, taking on one lesson at a time.

The book is organized as follows; Each Day begins with an **inspiring lyric** followed by a story of **a life lesson** from the author.

Beneath that is your **Affirmation of the Day**. Affirmations are statements or proclamations you can use to "call things into being" for your life. The dictionary defines affirmations as, "Something declared to be true; a positive statement or judgment." Simply put an affirmation is choosing your swagger. I encourage you to stand up tall and speak your daily affirmation out loud, repeating it three times. Some like to look in the mirror as they recite these words. Figure out what works for you as you go along.

Lastly, I have included the **Question of the Day**. These are designed to help lock-in the learning gained as you work with this book. These questions also provide you with an opportunity to reflect and capture your thoughts on the subject matter. Visit my blog (**runthepoint.blogspot.com)** where you can share your answers to the Question of the Day, see what others have written and interact with other readers. That's it!

Know the rules, understand them, and then break them.

Go ahead and move the crowd...your way.

Please visit our latest website: Hiiphopaffirmations.com

Where's Brooklyn At?

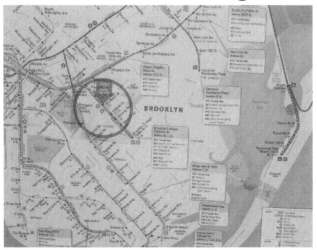

Photo credit: Run the Point Enterprises

Photo credit: Run the Point Enterprises

Day 1   Winning

"I will not lose."

Jay-Z

Confidence is everything. Belief in yourself can be a powerful tool forcing the universe to provide what you demand. But how do you build confidence?

For me it has been through preparation and a personal structure system that keeps me "in the zone." I have used "I will not lose," before public speaking, meetings with clients and when playing competitive sports. The statement or better yet the proclamation, "I will not lose," propels me into action mode. I've done all the preparation and practice I am going to do. It's time for me to believe in my training, my coaching and put it all together into a stunning performance.

Throughout graduate school I had what I called my lucky pair of shoes. There really wasn't anything lucky about them, but I built them up to be the shoes I put on before a big job interview or presentation. I would go around saying, "I've got my lucky shoes on. When you see these lucky shoes you know someone's in trouble... and it ain't me!" It is just one example of using a structure to keep you in the "frame of mind" you want to be in. If I was slipping into the world of doubt, I could look down at my shoes and "get my mind right." When my mind is right and I am in my zone, I can't lose.

Affirmation of the Day 1: I will not lose

Question of the Day 1: What structure or system do you use to motivate yourself to success?

Day 2   Your Music

"Sometimes we find peace in the beats and the breaks."

Common

Have you ever found yourself in a position where you just could not put together the words you were looking for to express how you were feeling? Music can be a tool to help you express your feelings. Whether it was a junior high school crush, using the lyrics from Kwame's "Sweet thing" or finding creative ways to express what my wife means to me with, "Make me better;" by Fabolous, music has helped me to talk to that special someone. Music has also helped to restore my brilliance when I could not see my future. Songs like Slick Rick's, "Hey young world," made me feel there was hope, "Go for yours, 'cause dreams come true." In addition, my memorization skills have been honed thanks to countless hours of memorizing songs so I could sing along at the next party.

Maybe you don't want to think about anything at all. Maybe you've had a bad day or maybe a bad week, but you know the right song to put you in a better mood. You don't care about lyrics at this point; you need a beat that will temporarily take your mind away from your current situation. There were many times when I've had to step away from being in the thick of things, relax with a song and let the creative problem solving energy come to me.

Affirmation of the Day 2: Today I discover the power of music and use it to reach new heights.

Question of the Day 2: How has music been a powerful tool in your life?

Visit **HipHopAffirmations.com**

Day 3   My Gift to the World

"Umi said shine your light on the world, shine your light for the world to see."

Mos Def

You know the words so sing with me: "This little light of mine, I'm gonna let it shine." Find your light or gift and put it to use. It does not have to be in a grand way at first.

Personally, I get excited when helping people clarify and achieve their goals. I decided to put that into practice by becoming a life coach. But how do you discover your light? One measure I use to identify my own light is what I call the "hair raising effect." You know the feeling; you are talking about a subject or are involved in a project that gives you goose bumps and gets you fired up. You have to pay attention to your senses and then take action with the goal of getting consistent results. Another step I take is to ask friends and associates to list what they think I am good at and what they might normally come to me for. I've even found myself experimenting in different arenas by doing volunteer or pro bono work.

Lastly, I simply spend time journaling and reflecting on experiences right after they have occurred. I look for patterns. I've found it interesting to look at what has worked and what has not worked for me over the past six to twelve months. Give it a try and see what you discover about yourself.

Affirmation of the Day 3: Today I discover my gift and use my gifts to benefit myself and others.

Question of the Day 3: If you were to ask 2 people from your private life and 2 people from your work life, what things you are good at, what might they say?

Day 4 - Vision

"I ain't looking at you dudes, I'm looking past you."

Jay-Z

Visionaries are often misunderstood. I define vision as something most people don't understand when first exposed to it. The person with vision is not excluded from the people who, "just don't get it" at first. That was the case for me when I began exploring professional life coaching. When I asked myself the age old question, "What is my purpose?" I found myself looking at all the things I love to do: helping people reach clarity, looking at things from different perspectives and restoring them back to their original state of brilliance so they can live the kind of life they want. I saw myself serving as a resource for those wanting to take themselves to the next level. I saw myself doing "it", but did not know quite how to articulate it. I shared it with a couple of people and they looked at me like I was crazy.

How do you define vision? You have to understand up front that what you see for yourself or your family may not be in line with what outsiders see. My suggestion; write down your vision, your ideas, your discoveries. It may not make any sense to you at first, but keep it anyway; you are going to need it later. I've personally kept a journal for years, and it always amazes me to go back and look at the recurring thoughts or themes in my life. Some ideas and thoughts I've had were just not ready to be implemented. Maybe I needed to mature or get new skills. Whatever the case, I believe in the old adage from the Bible, "When the student is ready the teacher will appear."

Hold on to your vision. Yes, some will tell you it's a crazy idea. Yes, some will tell you it will never work. In spite of that, get a supportive network, decide for yourself and keep the faith.

Affirmation of the Day 4: Today I will examine my recurring thoughts, dreams, ideas and visions.

Question of the Day 4: What visions have I had and not paid attention to?

Day 5 - Faith

"Just keep your faith in me, don't act impatiently; you'll get where you need to be in due time."

OutKast featuring Cee-Lo

I imagine my readers are of various faiths and backgrounds. What I offer here is my perspective on faith. I've had to be reminded that there is a force greater than myself at work every second of every minute of every day. "Do all you can and leave it in GOD's hands," I hear shouted out. This can be extremely difficult for some of us. I speak from experience; I have a tendency to worry about things that I cannot always influence. GOD has shown me time and time again that I have to do my part and allow GOD to do the rest, but I guess I am "hard headed" at times. I am not perfect, but I am better than I was. As of late I have learned to spend time on a daily basis meditating in order to quiet my mind as I prepare for the day.

Affirmation of the Day 5: I do not have all the answers, but I have faith in my abilities and a power greater than myself to guide me towards my goals.

Question of the Day 5: What is your perspective on faith?

Day 6 - Support

"I want to talk to GOD but I'm afraid because we ain't spoke in so long."

Kanye West

One of the toughest things I have found in my life is actually reaching out to someone when I really needed help. It can be quite a humbling experience to let down my guard and say, "Hey, I need some help." There have been a number of reasons why I did not seek the help I needed; there were times I did not know I needed help; there were times I thought I was supposed to know the answer; then there were times I received help and did not want to go back for more assistance.

You may relate to some of the reasons I've listed above. I have discovered that no one knows all the answers and nobody gets anywhere in life by themselves. Although you may think you have the answer, it behooves you to seek help. At a recent conference I attended, two major points stood out to me; Point #1, "If you already know how you are going to accomplish your goal, then it just isn't big enough." Point #2, "If you can accomplish your goal without assistance from others then your goals are probably too small." These two points are just a reminder that we all need assistance from time to time.

Affirmation of the Day 6: Today I ask for help in reaching my goals. Whether it is GOD, a mentor or a professional / expert, I will initiate contact to achieve success.

Question of the Day 6: How do you view asking for help?

Day 7 - Tribulation

"Life is a beautiful struggle, some people using their brain, some people using their muscle, some put it all together like a beautiful puzzle."

Talib Kwali

Life's beautiful struggle is to figure out our purpose... and live it. While attending a conference I had the pleasure of hearing Michael Lee Chin (Black Billionaire) speak. He gave one of the best definitions for the word "crisis," based on a definition from a Chinese dialect. He noted that the word crisis means danger and opportunity. We should not be surprised by the danger, as it is written in the Good Book that we will have tribulations in this life. However, we often spend so much time on the danger that we miss the opportunity. It is also written that we will never be given more than we can handle.

You have to use what you have, in order to get where you want to be. We all have been blessed with different talents. The key is the discovery process. Many situations labeled as failure really aren't. Finding out what you do not like is as powerful as finding out what you do like. Take every situation you find yourself in as an opportunity to discover something about yourself.

Affirmation of the Day 7: Today, I look at every situation as an opportunity to discover or use my talents.

Question of the Day 7: What crisis have you experienced that has enabled you to discover hidden talents?

Visit **HipHopAffirmations.com**

Day 8 - Listening

"I sell ice in the winter, fire in hell,
I'm a hustler baby, I sell water
to a well."

Jay-Z

Several weeks back I decided to have lunch with a college friend. I was in the process of building my coaching clientele and reaching out to many people. I wanted to let everyone know what I was up to and explore if they would be interested in sampling my services. I reached out to many and was not having too much success. I decided to meet with my college friend just to catch up and hear what was going on in his world. I knew he left a job not long ago and I figured he was already in another position.

The more I listened, the more I realized that my friend was at a stage in his life where he was not looking for the next job. Instead, he was looking for something that would be in alignment with his wants. Completely focusing on what he was sharing, I said, "I can help you." Until that point

I had not mentioned my work as a life coach. I focused on his needs and not my own. The opportunity naturally presented itself and it only made sense to work together to meet his needs.

How many times have you gone into a situation clear on what you wanted and tried to convince whoever you were talking to that they felt the same way? You were probably doing most of the talking. The next time you find yourself in that situation, take a breath and remember to proceed with this mindset; seek first to understand. Another helpful tip is the acronym WAIT. It stands for Why Am I Talking? Know what you want out of the situation you are in, but remember to learn what the other person is looking for and create a match between the two.

We excel when we have an understanding of what the other person wants or needs. It may sound obvious but the best way to find out is just to ask. You might also directly observe the situation. Do not rely on past experiences that may be similar; just ask the question, listen and act on what you find.

Affirmation of the Day 8: I can get everything I want by helping others get what they want.

Question of the Day 8: Where in your life would it be beneficial to ask another person, "What's important to you?"

Day 9   My Direction

"I'm a hustler baby, I just want you to know, it ain't where I been, but where I'm about to go."

Jay-Z

Where you from?(sic) This is a phrase we are very familiar with but it can have many different levels of meaning. "Where you from?" can mean, how far you think you can go in life or how you are supposed to act. Being the mild mannered person that I am (most of the time), I get a kick out of people who act surprised when I tell them I was born and raised in Brooklyn. The usual response is, "you don't sound like you're from Brooklyn." Or my favorite is the look of surprise, which I have learned to interpret as, "you don't **act** like you're from Brooklyn." I was absent the day they taught how to act and sound like a Brooklynite. What I was present for were the lessons I have learned on the streets and how to use those experiences to get where I want to go.

It's temporary in my mind and nothing is etched in stone. You are where you are for a short while so make the best of it. I remember relying on that thought many times as I worked as a concessionaire at a movie theatre. I smiled when customers where rude, knowing that this is only temporary, I have a bigger vision that keeps me going. For all the questions of where I'm from, very few people have ever asked me the question, "where are you going?"

Where are you going? Envision yourself where you want to be. Maybe you don't know where you want to be or what you want to do. That's okay; start dreaming. Start paying attention to what excites you. It might be inner peace you crave or it may be a BMW X5. Whatever it is, start seeing it in your life right now! Let that excite you no matter what your current situation is.

Affirmation of the Day 9: Where I am now is merely the starting point of where I'll end up.

Question of the Day 9: Where are you going?

Visit **HipHopAffirmations.com**

Day 10 - Opportunity

"You only get one shot, do not miss your chance to blow, opportunity comes once in a lifetime."

Eminem

Preparation is one of my strengths. I get prepared by asking questions and getting an understanding of what it takes to be "successful" at a particular task. I ask the question, what does success look like? Another question is, what does unbelievable success look like? On the other hand, a continued area of development for me is being ready. I always feel there is something else that needs to be done before I can move. One more "t" to cross or another "i" to dot. When this turns into delay this can lead to lost opportunities.

How do you prepare? Are you ready? If the answer is, "no," start working towards a "yes." How you prepare is practice, practice, practice and study, study, study. Learn your opponent and what it takes to become victorious. In your life, the opponent may be an exam, a budget, a work assignment, a project at home or something else you want to conquer.

What does a state of readiness look like? Picture an athlete with knees and elbows bent standing on the balls of their feet. The athlete may display a little bit of rocking motion so they are already in motion and can react to whatever happens. They are calm and ready to seize opportunity in what may seem like chaos to spectators. I try to keep this picture in mind when everything around me is going crazy.

Affirmation of the Day 10: I am prepared and ready for opportunity!

Question of the Day 10: Similar to the athlete what does your state of readiness look like?

Visit **HipHopAffirmations.com**

Day 11 – Progress

"I ain't no perfect man, I'm trying to do the best that I can with what it is I have."

Mos Def

Work in progress is the sign I should have hanging from my chest. I sometimes forget that I still have to keep moving despite my imperfection. I've wasted too much time trying to be perfect or avoiding the perception of being viewed as "not perfect," by others. This book you are reading right now is a perfect example (no pun intended). It has been in my heart and head for a number of years. How is it going to get published, what songs will I use, and whose help do I need? All questions of static perfection. I decided to move forward with the two things I knew for sure; lyrics move me and I find something positive in what can be viewed in a negative light. That's it; anything to get the process going.

So what are you waiting for? Let me help you out. "You are not perfect and folks will talk about you no matter what you do." Now that we've got that out of the way, let's move forward. I believe there is nothing wrong with striving towards perfection, but just don't allow it to stop you from moving at all. Using perfection in a way that motivates you to move towards something that isn't in existence yet is what I refer to as active perfection. Being stuck in a place where you do not take action because everything must be perfect is what I call static perfection. You have to understand you are capable of doing amazing things from where you are right now. You are smart enough, beautiful enough and bold enough to realize your dreams right now. Use the energy, vision and passion from your active perfection as a roadmap to get you moving towards what you want and keep you moving in good and bad times, times of total clarity and times of utter confusion. The question is, "Will you focus on static or active perfection in your life?"

Affirmation of the Day 11: I use the gifts I have to strive towards perfection.

Question of the Day 11: What does active perfection look like in your life?

Day 12 – Love

"It's easy to love me now. Would you love me if I was down and out? Would you still have love for me?"

50 Cent

When I wasn't doing the right thing as a youngster in high school, my dad did not look at it as a phase. He looked at it as unacceptable according to his standards and the standards he wanted for our family. He did not give me a beating as you might expect from a Haitian parent, but instead he looked me straight in the eyes and said, "If you want to continue on the path that you are heading, that is your choice, you are old enough to know right from wrong (I was 14). I ask only one favor. Don't say anything to me when you see me in the street or in this house." I did not need a beating, those words hurt me more than any physical blow he could have given me. Yet, I knew his words came from a place of love for me.

Would you still love me if I was down and out? Ask around and the answer to the question may be, "yes," but the way that love is expressed may not always be the way we expect. There are at least two perspectives on loving someone when they are down and out that I have seen. We can be held and coddled at our low point, or we can be lifted out with a kick in the butt and a reminded of how great we truly are and can be; even in our down and out phase.

The first perspective is to mentally go to a place of feeling down and out. We can believe it is okay to stay there. In this situation the focus is on what has gone wrong. We have a feeling of sympathy when we see others there. We feel the pain the person is experiencing. There is a sense of pity. You might say; "I hope they get out of it."

The second perspective is to spend a limited time in that place of feeling down and out. When a person is in this situation we can show compassion and then help them move on. At first this might seem insensitive and even harsh, but with further inspection it's a sign of love for the person and belief in the great person they can be. We decide not to be patient and not to settle for mediocrity. The thought of loving "you" revolves around holding yourself to a higher standard to be the best you, you can be. In this space there is a sense that the situation is separate from the person and the person is bigger than the situation.

Having people love you no matter where you are in your life is extremely important. They are there to comfort and nurture you. We also need people to provide the kind of love that sometimes hurts; to hold us to task and keep us accountable for our greatness. We need people who have a certain standard for themselves and propel us to have higher standards for ourselves.

Affirmation of the Day 12: I love myself and others with high standards.

Question of the Day 12: What kind of love has worked best for you?

Visit **HipHopAffirmations.com**

Day 13 Preconceived Notion

"The Martha Stewart that's far from Jewish; far from a Harvard Student, just had the balls to do it."

Jay-Z

I remember sharing my post college goals about wanting to work with the Olympics in event management. I told a woman, who thought it was her duty to stop me from dreaming. Instead, she wanted me to focus on her reality. I was not 100% sure of her intent, but I think she might have thought I was being too cocky or confident. I was mentally living in the world of abundance. It was not the same place she was coming from. She told me that GOD has a way of humbling us. I did not think much of it then, but upon reflection, I know GOD wants me to, "have life and have it more abundantly."

You might have a preconceived definition of what you must have or look like to be successful. You do not have to subscribe to that thought. Experiment and find out what works for you and take bold steps towards what you want. Do the research and you will find there are successful people of all walks of life, from every race, sex, religion and description. It is easy to list the reasons why your dreams may not be possible but I challenge you to study the life of someone with a similar background or situation as yourself, who has accomplished the kind of success you desire.

Have confidence in who you are and worry less about who you are not. If you listen to the critics or haters, you will never be good enough, smart enough, fast enough or - fill in the blank - enough to accomplish your goals. If it only takes one person to change your mind, then know that I support you.

Affirmation of the Day 13: I can be successful by being me.

Question of the Day 13: What are the prerequisites of success in your mind?

Day 14   Your Mindset

"How could you falter when you're the rock of Gibraltar; I had to get off the boat so I could walk on water."

Jay-Z

My high school football coach had a unique way of getting us to push pass our limits. He introduced us to, "The little man on our shoulder." It was a mythical figure that stood on our shoulder telling us that we would not accomplish the task at hand. He taught us to physically brush the little man off our shoulder and move forward to accomplish the things we needed to get done. So before Jay-Z told us to "go 'head brush your shoulder off" my high school coach had us doing that same move. Thanks coach App. He knew we could not get where we really wanted or needed to be by staying in our comfort zone. We had to get pass what we knew and had accomplished already.

Have you ever seen the t-shirt that reads, "I do what the voices in my head tell me?" I used to laugh at the shirt until I realized that it is true. There is a little voice that tells us that we are not ready, we need more information, and asks: "how are we going to get that done?" That voice suggests that maybe we should wait and offers a host of other self limiting messages. There is another voice that says, "You are meant to do great things." I prefer the latter. These voices can help or hinder us in reaching our natural greatness. Your mind must change to reach your greatness. Just like stopping at a gas station and asking for directions to a remote location after veering off-course; you may not be able to get there from here. You have to make a couple of turns and adjustments before you will be on your way to where you want to be.

Affirmation of the Day 14: I brush the little man off my shoulder, enabling me to move forward to my destiny.

Question of the Day 14: What is the little man on your shoulder telling you can't be done in your life?

Day 15   Your True Self

*"You only know what you see, you
don't understand what it takes to
be me."*

Jay-Z

Or should I say, "You don't understand what it
took to be me." How many times have you been
robbed on the way from school (with or without
a gun, you choose one)? How many times have
you had your bike stolen? Boy, I wish I knew
about tax write-offs and insurance back then.
How many times have you sat up in the middle of
the night crying in your mom's kitchen because
you could not see your next move? College?...
Where am I gonna get money for that? How
many times have you been told you are hanging
out with the wrong crowd and they are nothing
but bad news? How many times have you had a
coach tell you that you have a lot of options and
places you can play football, it's not just D-I out
there. How many times have you had a random
crackhead see you walking with your head down
and said, "keep your head up." How many

31

times have you told your mentor on his birthday (coincidence) that you just accepted Jesus Christ as your personal Savior to get the response; "You did not accept him today, he accepted you."

The person that you see before you is a composite of many different experiences both good and bad. There is no way I could have planned the variety of experiences that have brought me to who I am today. In fact, I'm still being shaped as we speak. The great thing is that I have discovered that my experiences, the people I am around, and the things I learn are impacted by daily decisions I make; even those that seem mundane.

Have you ever felt like no one understands you? That they only know what is on the surface? As human beings we are all complex creatures. Just like the ice bergs of the arctic, what people see or perceive is only a small fraction of what we really have to offer. 10% is visible; 90% is under water and unseen.

Our complexity has taught me two things: first, you have to be patient with people to get to know who they really are. One action does not define them. Second, most people are looking for the opportunity to reveal themselves. Try and create an environment that is not judgmental and encourages openness. You must lead by example by revealing yourself.

Affirmation of the Day 15: Today I embrace the multi-faceted nature of my being.

Question of the Day 15: What part of you would you like to express more?

Visit **HipHopAffirmations.com**

Day 16 - Stress

"I really know how it feels to be stressed out, stressed out. When you're face to face with your adversity."

A Tribe Called Quest

In high school I picked up a phrase, "no stress." I used it to replace such phrases as, "don't worry about it, (e.g. someone steps on your foot by accident—'no stress'. Someone says they will be running a little late—"no stress.") I said it because I thought it was unique, but after a while I realized two things; first, people were identifying me with the phrase and second, some people started using it as a reminder for themselves, not to sweat the small stuff, with the realization that it's all small stuff.

Personally, when things are feeling too stressful, there are several things I do or at least strive to do. First is pray, second is plan, third is take action, fourth is look for positive interactions with people. I strive to pray first, but it doesn't always happen that way. I get caught in the heat of the moment and go right into planning or trying to take some kind of action.

We all have moments of stress in our lives. Some stress motivates us and some deters progress. How do you handle it or use it to your advantage? Do you have a ritual for de-stressing? Do you have a place you can go to help reduce the stress in your life?

Accepting that we will have stressful situations in life, puts us one step closer to reaching peace of mind.

Affirmation of the Day 16: No stress; I accept stress as part of my life and create concrete ways to deal with it.

Question of the Day 16: How do you handle stress?

Day 17 - Attitude

"If I can't do it, homie it can't be done."

50 Cent

Entering a situation with the right attitude can make all the difference in your daily activities. The right attitude or should I say a positive attitude can create an aura about you which will attract the things and people you need to accomplish your goals. Throughout my journey I have kept an eye out for things and people that bring out the best in me. I have a need for structure so I have created a way to work with what motivates me to move forward confidently. I usually like to take a couple of minutes of silence where I can gather my energy, recite one of my favorite poems, "Somebody said it couldn't be done," envision the result I want and then get after it.

Make a mental note to yourself, there will be people around you who sing a different song, "I or you can't do it homie." You may want to acknowledge their belief, but please don't adopt it. In a world filled with inner and external doubt, fight through and believe in "you." When you use your positive spirit to accomplish things, however small, it creates momentum for even more things to get done. It also provides energy to those around you. Make the decision to be the catalyst. Use the momentum generated to boost your confidence and make even more things happen.

Affirmation of the Day 17: I can do it, it can be done.

Question of the Day 17: What was the last situation that you experienced where "fighting through and believing in you," made the difference?

Day 18   Being Worthy

"Whose world is this, the world is yours, the world is yours...it's mine, it's mine, it's mine."

NAS

.

No one and I mean no one in my life lives by the above principle more than my wife. On first appearances or meeting she would be described as a quiet Asian (Korean to be specific) woman. Getting to really know her you would quickly find out that she is a woman who knows what she wants and what she deserves. The answer to both what she wants and deserves is the very best. She is not limited by what she personally knows how to do. Instead, she is motivated by what she wants; and she wants big. For example, back when we were planning our wedding, my main focus was on how much everything was going to cost, not the experience we were going to have. I was not focused on the fact that this was something we were only going to do once, til death do us part. My vision was to have a service at any location and have a reception at any location.   Not good enough for my bride to be. She wanted to get married in a castle. And guess what?...We made it happen. Things started lining up and the necessary people started to come into our lives. I do not believe this would have happened if we did not make the commitment to go for it and go for it big. Every time I look at our wedding pictures I am in awe of how it all came together. I also look at it as a lesson reminding me not to let my current situation serve as the platform I use to dream from. Basically, if you know all of the details around how you are going to get your big dream accomplished, then it is just not big enough, period. I have learned so much about living beyond my limitations thanks to my wife. One thing I have learned about myself is that I often allow what I want to be based on what I know I can have. This is a significantly limiting mindset. The change did not come easy and I occasionally struggle with getting stuck in what I know or what I have seen as reference points to what I think I can have.

How often do you let details and your current situation stop you from dreaming big? Let's be real...are you one of the people who say, "I don't want to be rich," just because you don't know how you are going to do it? Do you say, "Money isn't everything," and use it as an excuse not to stretch yourself and try new things that could bring you, your family and your cause(s) money? I suggest you take a shift in attitude, if only for a moment and see what it feels like. Test drive a car that you think is totally out of your league. Go and visit a couple of open houses in an affluent area next Sunday. Set up an informational interview with the company you want to work for (don't know how? Email me and I'll coach you through it: bruny@runthepoint.com). Change the way you respond when people greet you (no more, "I'm Just surviving"). You will start to see things come together to help you move towards getting what you desire. You may not get the Bentley coup, but striving for it will move you out of your current comfort zone which is an accomplishment in itself.

Affirmation of the Day 18: I believe that I am worthy of great things.

Question of the Day 18: What would you attempt to do if you knew you could not fail?

Visit **HipHopAffirmations.com**

My wife and I on our wedding day

Photo credit: Joel Louis

Day 19   Make the Change

"It's cool to look bummy, be a dumb dummy and disrespect your mummy."

Slick Rick

I'll never forget my freshman year of high school. I really thought it was cool to look bummy, be a dumb, dummy and disrespect my mummy(sic). Don't get me wrong, I went to school everyday, but I never went to class. I roamed the halls, courtyard or jumped on the train heading to a hooky party. A hooky party was a party that was held during school hours. It usually took place at some unsuspecting working parent(s)' home (a working parent who thought their son or daughter was home sick that day, but instead decided to have a couple of friends over).

I'll never forget receiving "cutting cards" sent to my house listing all the classes I skipped. Envision an index card; one side listing all of the classes I skipped and concluding with "Continued on back." The back continued to list classes I missed. The bottom of the card read, "Too many to list." My mom took it as a phase that I was going through, but my dad on the other hand flipped when he found out my grades plummeted, I was hanging out with the wrong crowd and I came home with a fake earring. His reaction was to ask me not to speak with him if I decided to continue on this path. That coupled with the fear of what my future would look like if I continued to do the same things I was doing caused me to make a change.

I went to night school, summer school and would have gone to night school in the summer if it was offered. All this so I could graduate in four years, after taking the first year as a sabbatical to fool around. I found two things I loved more than my peeps; myself and my Dad. "Thanks Pop (R.I.P)"

Do you follow the crowd at the expense of yourself or do you lead the crowd to do the right things? I know it is not always easy to deal with being popular and trying to do the right. True popularity and leadership calls for you to be a little bit different. It calls for you to follow what you know is right and true for you. As you explore and make new discoveries in your life, know that things are going to change. The people you hang out with may change, your wardrobe may change, the things that you have come to take as absolute truths may change. Be open and don't ignore the new discoveries that could have a dramatic impact on your life.

Affirmation of the Day 19: I am aware of my actions and the impact they can have on my future. I look to my future self as a way of checking alignment towards my goal.

Question of the Day 19: What did or will it take for you to make a change in your life?

Visit **HipHopAffirmations.com**

Day 20 - Rejection

"So when I blow up, don't try and kick it to me later."

Positive K

Rejection is part of life whether we like it or not. Where is the opportunity in rejection? I recall back when I just got out of graduate school and was looking for a job. I had my hopes on a position with a sports conference and was fairly confident that I would get it. Days passed and I finally got word that I did not get the position. They told me it was very close, but the other person had a certain qualification that I did not. I moved on to an internship and by the end of my internship I was contacted by the same conference to apply for another position that became available. Once again, it was a tough decision for them to make, but they went with the other candidate. I was destroyed because this was really the first time in my life I had to deal with this type of rejection and I really took it personally. I called one of my mentors and told them the situation. He did not have an ounce of sympathy for me. Instead, I was asked, "Do you know where the person who accepted the job came from?" I quickly said, "No." They responded by saying, "That's too bad, because if they left their old job for this new job, there's an opportunity to fill their old position." A totally different perspective on the situation.

How do you handle rejection? Are you totally destroyed and get down on yourself or do you look for the opportunity in the situation? Decide that you will be big, i.e. "blow up" and rejection is only preparing you for something better. As emotional as getting rejected can be, try to see what there is to learn or gain from the situation.

Affirmation of the Day 20: Rejection is an opportunity for reflection.

Question of the Day 20: How do you handle rejection?

Visit **HipHopAffirmations.com**

Day 21 - Worry

"Did you ever think that you would be this rich? Did you ever think that you would be this paid?"

R.Kelly / Nas

I want to yell out, "Yeah" to the statement above, but that has not always been true. I do not always have unwavering faith as I strive to accomplish my goals. I've had my share of being, "shook" and not sure how things are going to work out. No matter how many times I've pulled through, I still find myself LOW (Leaning On Worry). Oh, me of little faith.

You name it, there has been some state of worry involved; how am I going to pay for college, am I ever going to find a job after graduate school, how can we afford to buy a house? There are many more examples, but the default has been to worry, at least a little, before calming myself down and remembering a couple of key things. First, if I have done all I can, then it's out of my hands. Second, if my goals don't spark some kind of worry, then they probably aren't big enough and I may be playing it too safe. With that being said, when I find myself worrying I have learned to take the opportunity to get curious and explore what I am concerned about.

How do you handle worry? Have you found a way to accept it as part of your life and don't allow it to bother you? Do you not worry at all because of your faith? However you handle it, know that worry is there as a defensive mechanism trying to protect you from what is perceived as a dangerous situation. By worrying you are subconsciously saying, "I better pay attention to this item." Here are a couple of suggestions to keep your worry in check: 1. make a list of the things that are worrying you. Sometimes writing it down and getting it out of your head is enough to stop your worrying. 2. Talk to someone you trust about what is on your mind. It's amazing how other folks can help us put our worry in perspective and think about things in ways we just would not have of on our own.

Another suggestion is to plant your feet firmly in the ground and just get to work.

Affirmation of the Day 21: I think big and big things happen.

Question of the Day 21: How could you use worrying to propel you into action towards your goal?

Day 22   Passion / Driven

"Treat my first like my last, and my last like my first."

Jay-Z

I recall hearing the story of Duke Ellington, the famous jazz musician, when asked by reporters, "Duke, you have composed so many great hits, which one is your favorite?" Duke answered, "My next one." Here was a man that although he reached a certain level of success and accomplishment, knew he still had more to create. He refused to rest on his past success.

Fears or rewards are two of the things that naturally cause us to make changes. In my life I have found myself using a combination of both to keep me going. For example, when I played college football, I worked very hard during the off season to get ready for the fall. I would imagine myself on the field knocking passes and people down (I was a Free Safety). My sophomore year I was given the chance to do just that. I became the starting Free Safety. I knew if I continued to work hard I would reach that point (reward). I also knew if I did not continue to work hard I could easily be replaced (fear). I played Division-III football so I decided to train with a Division-I strength trainer in the summer. Every year it felt like there was some new kid who was going to come in and take my spot (hey, I did it to someone else).The mixture of fear and reward motivated me to look for ways to continually get better. I knew and implemented the summer training strategy we were given and I also did a little extra.

How do you continue to feed the passion inside of you? Remember how it felt to work like you owned the job as an intern. Compare that to working as hard as an intern when you finally earned that full time position. What's the difference between the two scenarios? Most interns usually have two things that can easily be lost as you become a seasoned veteran. The first is passion and a kind of, "Hey I've got nothing to lose" attitude and the second is curiosity. I invite you to explore the two over the next couple of days. What are you passionate about in your current situation? What's a different perspective you could take on your current situation? Use your answers as a launching pad whenever you find yourself stuck or in a rut.

Affirmation of the Day 22: Today I attack whatever challenge I face with enough energy to make something happen.

Question of the Day 22: What are you passionate about in your current situation?

Day 23 Time Management

"The truth is time waits for none of you; in fact he can't wait for the date to snatch the ground right from under you."

Nas

Don't ask me how I did it, but while in college, I was literally involved in everything. That includes staying up all night to study for exams, waking up at 7:00 a.m. and going into town to experience St. Patty's day, playing football, running track, acting, serving as a peer counselor, mentor, spending at least 2hrs per night in the library, being a founding father for a chapter of my multicultural fraternity (Gamma Omega Delta Fraternity, Inc.) and courting my future wife. I made up my mind that I did not want to just go to college, I wanted to experience it. I knew I was there for a short time and I wanted to get the most I could out of it; I only had 4 years.

What if I approached the rest of my life with such awareness of the limited amount of time I'm given on this earth? It would provide a sense of focus that is easily lost once done with school and faced with THE REST OF MY LIFE.

There are times when we procrastinate or just don't do things that we know we should, thinking we can do it tomorrow. According to Benjamin Franklin, "Never put off 'til tomorrow what you can do today." How would you treat your life if you knew how long you would live? What if you only had 10 years to live, would your actions still be the same? Start building a plan towards the things you know you want to do in your lifetime. Don't wait or think that you will have tomorrow. Create a list of 100 things you have to do in your lifetime and start to act on that list. As you complete them, cross them off your list. You will be amazed at how many things you can accomplish when you write them down. Your mind will take a picture of what you want to do and before you know it, you will have accomplished many of the things on your list.

Don't wait until tomorrow, get started today! Take it to another level and swap lists with someone you trust and schedule to meet with them every 6 to 12 months to check-in on each other's progress.

Affirmation of the Day 23: My time is valuable and I treat it that way.

Question of the Day 23: What are some of the things on your list that you want to be held accountable for?

Day 24 - Change

*"Everybody looking strange, saying,
'you changed.' Like you worked
that hard so you can stay
the same."*

Jay-Z

Ah, yes, the only constant is change. No matter how much we try and fight it, change is inevitable. We have the option of being a force that tries to stop it, tries to lead it or be a part of it. Why do parents work so hard to give their children a better life? Why do individuals / groups look for ways to elevate themselves and those around them? It is all to make a positive change; to have more, to be more, to give more.

In my life I have had the internal struggle of wanting to "keep it real" and simultaneously wanting to be more then just a kid from Brooklyn who stayed in the hood and hung out in front of the building. That was just my personal desire (not to degrade anyone else). I've struggled with the fact that I wanted to make money and make lots of it while living a spiritual life. Are the two contradictory? "No!" To take a quote from the motivational speaker Zig Ziglar, "I believe GOD made the diamonds for his bunch, not Satan's crowd."

Have no guilt about wanting to achieve success. There is nothing glorious about poverty. I recall one of my mentors teaching me the honor in wanting to save the world, but being sure you take care of yourself so you can actually do it. You cannot help others if you are not in a good place to help yourself. BE the change you want to see.

I have a friend whose PhD work focused on African-American males not using their intellectual talents for fear of being considered "uncool" or nerdy. They sacrifice the full college experience in exchange for not "selling out."

Unfortunately, they are actually "selling out" their full potential and experience(s).

Next time someone confronts you with, "You've changed" simply smile and respond, "the issue is not that I have changed, but that you have not."

Affirmation of the Day 24: I make the necessary changes needed to be and have what I dream.

Question of the Day 24: What change can you make in your life that will have the biggest impact right now?

Day 25 Personal Expression

"You know I only say it 'cause I'm truly genuine; don't be a hard rock when you really are a gem."

Lauren Hill

"Express yourself," said the late godfather of soul, James Brown. You can try and suppress your deep feelings, but they have a way of finding a form of expression. Learn to deal with it up front.

For a long time I had an internal issue with anger. I really did not know how to express what I was feeling. Something would not go my way and then I would become disengaged and silent. At the end of my silent spell, I would realize that what or who I was upset with just wasn't worth it. I did not know how to get back and apologize for being withdrawn. As time went on, I learned to express my anger, disappointment or frustration when it happened. That allowed me to move on with my day. Open communication, no matter what, is what worked for me. I also started hiking. Becoming one with nature gave me a sense of peace and calmness. It gave me time to be more reflective and to get a sense of what is really important.

One of my personal forms of expression is dancing. I've been doing it as long as I could remember. It goes back to hooky parties in the basements of Brooklyn homes (hip hop and reggae) to salsa and merengue in the Dominican Republic. Dancing helps me to express my creativity, harmony and attitude. What's your personal form of expression? Do you write, sing, paint or dance? Whatever it is, embrace it and allow it to fill and refresh your spirit.

Affirmation of the Day 25: I am open to my creative possibilities.

Question of the Day 25: How do you personally express yourself?

Day 26   Decision Making

"Just know that I chose my own fate, I drove by the fork in the road and went straight."

Jay-Z

What are the driving forces that allow you to choose one thing over another? In my life it has been several things: my faith in GOD, my internal compass and most recently, values - based decision making. Each of these has helped me in times when I just did not know which direction to go. My faith in GOD has allowed me to be still long enough to get a sense of what he would have me do and to affirm that whatever the future holds, I am in good hands. I will not pretend that this has been easy nor will I suggest that I have not spent too much time pondering the possibilities for the future. My internal compass, or gut, is another form that has assisted me when it was time to make daily decisions . Currently, my work as a life coach provides a focused view on my values and how I can live them more fully and more often.

How do you make decisions? If you are a person of faith, I suggest that you recite the following scripture (the word "you" has been replaced with "I" to personalize it), "Faith is being sure of what I hope for and certain of things I have not seen." If you are a gut person, I suggest you actually name your gut and set up time to consult with him/her on a regular basis. I think you will be surprised how many answers are already inside of you. You can start with questions like, what do I really want in this situation?, what's most important in this situation? and what if I thought about this in a really BIG way and knew I could not fail?.

For those of you who are interested in making more decisions based on your values, I suggest you list them and review them on a daily or weekly basis to see how you are holding yourself accountable. Using a rating system from 1-10 (1 being you are not living those values at all to 10 being you are living those values fully). Put at least one of these into practice and watch how alive you become as you start to live in on purpose, not waiting for decisions to be made for you.

Affirmation of the Day 26: I make my decisions based on what is truly important to me.

Question of the Day 26: What guides your decision making process?

Day 27 - Focus

"I'm focused man."

Jay-Z

As a kid I had a lot of energy and not much focus. I used to quickly finish my school work and stop the rest of the students from completing theirs. I probably would have been diagnosed with Attention Deficiency Disorder if it wasn't for my uncle Dr. Leslie Moliere (R.I.P) who had my mom take me off some medication that took me from being super hyper to totally lethargic. Now back to the present day... For me to get into a state of focus it sometimes takes steps that can seem redundant or unorthodox. First, to get focused I like to put myself in a position to work. That means although I do most of my coaching and writing from home, as soon as I get up and it's time to get into work mode, I throw on a dress shirt. I may still have my PJ pants on, but in my mind the dress shirt makes it official. I also have little things like a thinking hat and glasses with no lens to give me a sense of being studious. Second, If I find myself slipping or being unproductive, I change my work location. I will go from my office upstairs to the kitchen table, To my second office in the basement. All this in search of the right place and environment for my focus and creativity (Just a note this may drive your spouse crazy as they try to keep a sense of peace and order).

How do you get and stay focused? Try visualizing the end result that you want and get excited about the thought of getting it done. Use that energy to get things going for you. Also, don't hesitate to put on some music if it helps you get into a groove, no pun intended. Another technique you can use is to step away from what you are working on when you find yourself drifting and begin to brainstorm possible ways to move forward. Here is one format that I use: List the project you are working on, the purpose (why you're doing it in the first place), the vision (what will it look like when you are done), brainstorm a couple of action items and lastly, organize those steps based on what needs to happen first, second, etc.

Affirmation of the Day 27: I'm focused man.

Question of the Day 27: How do you get and stay focused? Or where is your place of greatest focus?

Day 28   A Fulfilling Life

The whole world lookin' at me; watchin and waitin to see if I fulfill my destiny."

Busta Rhymes

At the first vision party (party where participants were asked to come dressed and in the mentality of who they want to be in 10yrs) held by my company Run the Point Enterprises, I had a speaker present who spoke about thinking big and how he has handled the ups and downs of being an entrepreneur. He said something very interesting that I don't think we often ponder. He said he was trying to be the best and biggest success he could be so he could help people in a big way. He used the analogy of being on an airplane going down in a crash; you are instructed to put on your air mask before you try to help anyone else with theirs. Why? Because if you are not breathing then you really can't help anyone else. That aligns with the thought of being as successful as you can, so you can give in a bigger way. I must confess that this is a fairly new way for me to look at things. I created a connection between helping and staying poor. I don't think it's a true connection; I believe lack of self confidence, guidance and not knowing how to become a big success can lead us to call our biggest vision of success sour grapes. We don't really want it, because we think we can't have it.

Do you view financial success as being within your grasp? The first thing you can do is to start dreaming. Imagine what you want to be and want to have as if it has already happened. Find magazines, books or places that inspire you to be the person you most want to be. The second thing you can do is find a mentor or guide who has been down the path you want to travel. My wife and I took a ride on a four-wheel motor bike while in the Dominican Republic. It's something I always wanted to do and we did it. We could have just gone around trying to find our way on the four-wheelers, but instead we had a guide (someone who knew the area, the coolest sights to see and the potholes to avoid). Let a mentor serve as your guide. Third, know that you will run into setbacks so build a structure that helps you get out of the valleys of your life. I suggest finding the songs, poetry, quotes and people that bring out the best in you.

Affirmation of the Day 28: I bring all of me to every situation and live a fulfilling life.

Question of the Day 28: What's your dream?

Visit **HipHopAffirmations.com**

Photo credit: Run The Point Enterprises

Day 29   Staying Positive

"How you gonna win, when you ain't right within?"

Lauren Hill

Let's ponder the potential answer to the question above. How do we assess when we are not right within? For me, I've learned to trust my internal gauge of who I want to be. The question for me has been, '"Is this the kind of man I want to be?" If the person I see in my internal gauge is not who I want to be, then a change is needed.

Let's say you get exactly what you want, but the method you use is not the most positive. You stepped on some folks to get it or weren't the most honest along the way. You feel a bit of unease from your conscious. Think about being a grandparent and telling your story to the grandkids. Are you proud of the things you did or the way you recovered from the things you did? What example have you created for the future generations? I believe you can still win and be right within. Go for it.

Affirmation of the Day 29: The actions I take are positive and benefit me on the outside and inside.

Question of the Day 29: What internal gauge do you use?

My form of expression as a youth in Brooklyn... "Nomad"

Photo Credits: Run the Point Enterprises

Day 30   Transferable Skills

"Everything I'm not, made me everything I am."

Kanye West

If I look back at all the mischievous things I did as a kid, it's a miracle that I wrote this book. I recall doing everything from stealing clothes, "boosting," from department stores to writing graffiti (see previous page for a sample) on trains and street walls. I had to make a shift not only because I did not want to get arrested but because I knew I wanted more than what those things had to offer in the long run. I took the positive transferable skills from my past to step up my game in the future. The planning and attention that goes into "boosting" clothes is now applied to managing events and brainstorming ideas. The variety of people I spent time with doing the wrong things taught me the skills to get along with a diverse group of individuals.

What did you have to give up to grow your game? The key is not to totally abandon what you used to do, but find how you can apply the positive skills in those acts to step up your game. What transferable skills can you take with you? What skills can you extract from your past to create opportunities in your future? In the bigger picture your bad habit (such as boosting) may have been in your life to help you gain the necessary skills to be where you currently are. No matter where you find yourself there is a lesson to be learned. Are you open?

Affirmation of the Day 30: I will use all of my experiences both positive and negative to my advantage.

Question of the Day 30: What transferable skills have you taken for granted?

Visit **runthepoint.blogspot.com**

Products and Services

Professional Life / Success Coaching

"There's got to be a better way, I know I'm better than this, I don't know my purpose, I need help getting unstuck. I find myself in the same situations over and over again. I just want more out of life." If any of the above describes you, **Ambassador Bruny** can help. As a **certified professional life coach** it is his pleasure to help you understand where you are, where you want to be and help you create a way to get there. The end results are clarity to make better decisions, being more marketable and being more profitable. His work begins from the platform that you are naturally Creative, Resourceful and Whole.

- **Your Essence Coaching Program:** 3 step process to rediscovering your values and using them for better decision making and goal setting.

Public Speaking / Workshop Facilitation

- **7 Days of Hip Hop Affirmation to Change Your Life (Series):** There is a workshop designated for H.S., College, Young Professionals and Student-Athletes. Ambassador Bruny uses the popular medium of hip hop combined with his life lessons to deliver an engaging presentation / workshop leaving your audience with tangible "Moves to Make," to increase their chances of success and reaching their goals.

- **Quarter Life Answer:** Workshops focused on helping young adults through the quarter life challenge. We focus on such topics as Networking, Mentoring, Overcoming self doubt and discovering your purpose. These workshops help young adults from age 25-35 become more marketable, gain clarity to make better life and professional decisions.

- **Vision Board Sessions:** Create the future you want by using a poster board to capture where and what you would like in your life in the next 5-10yrs. Use crayons, markers and pictures from your favorite magazines to create a visual stimulus to keep you on the path towards your goals.

About the Author

Mike "Ambassador" Bruny was born and raised in the Flatbush section of Brooklyn, New York to Haitian parents. In his everyday life Mike serves as an ambassador to people's highest vision of themselves.

Mike runs a professional and personal coaching practice focused mainly on helping young adults through life transitions. He helps them become more marketable, gain clarity and focus on their most important goals through his professional life/success coaching programs. His clients have described him as insightful, passionate and committed to their highest vision.

Mike is a Certified Professional Co-active Coach, receiving his training through The Coaches Training Institute (CTI). Mike has an undergraduate degree in Psychology from Hartwick College, a Masters in Sports Management from the University of Massachusetts, Amherst and is an alumnus of The Partnership, Inc. in Boston, MA. He is a former collegiate athlete, excelling in Football and Track. He spends time volunteering in the career development ministry and the men's retreat committee at his church.

Mike held executive positions in athletics at Syracuse University, the University of Connecticut and New Balance Athletic shoes. He traveled around the country as a professional speaker for Monster's Making it Count Program. Some of his other speaking clients included the WNBA (Women's National Basketball Association), Hartwick College, Greater Framingham Community Church, INROADS, Columbia University Athletics, Raytheon, The Jericho Project, Phoenix Charter Academy, MetLife, WPI, Clark University, and, SUNY Oneonta Framingham State College to name a few.

Mike can be reached by:
Web: www.hiphopaffirmations.com
Email: Bruny@hiphopaffirmations.com
Phone: 617-943-1417

Facebook:

www.facebook.com/hiphopaffirmations

Twitter: @hiphopaffirms

Youtube: www.youtube.com/ambassadorbruny

Made in the USA
San Bernardino, CA
03 September 2015